Something
BIG

Susan Rose Simms

LIFESKILLS IN ACTION
MONEY SKILLS

 MONEY

Living on a Budget | Road Trip
Opening a Bank Account | The Guitar
Managing Credit | High Cost
Using Coupons | Get the Deal
Planning to Save | Something Big

LIVING

Smart Grocery Shopping | Shop Smart
Doing Household Chores | Keep It Clean
Finding a Place to Live | A Place of Our Own
Moving In | Pack Up
Cooking Your Own Meals | Dinner Is Served

JOB

Preparing a Résumé
Finding a Job
Job Interview Basics
How to Act Right on the Job
Employee Rights

SADDLEBACK
EDUCATIONAL PUBLISHING
www.sdlback.com

ISBN-13: 978-1-68021-013-2
ISBN-10: 1-68021-013-0
eBook: 978-1-63078-297-9

Printed in Malaysia

20 19 18 17 16   2 3 4 5 6

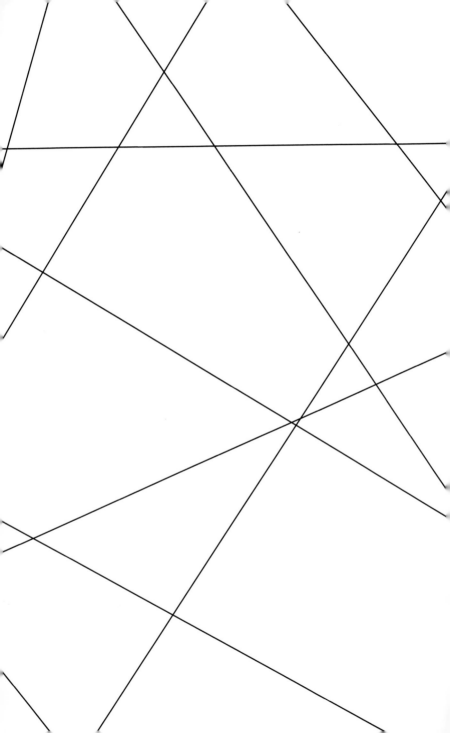

The bell rang. Students raced to class.
Summer was over. A new year of high
school had begun.

Zach and Zoe had economics first period.
They were twins. But they were nothing alike.

"Good morning, class," said Ms. Sands.
"Let's talk about your term project."

Everyone was quiet. Zach sat in the front
row. His eyes were on Ms. Sands. Zoe sat
in back. She was daydreaming about her
summer.

"For your project this term …" Ms. Sands paused. Then she smiled. "You will each have $500."

Mouths fell open. "For real?" Eddie called out.

"Not real money," said Ms. Sands. "But it will really count. This project is 40% of your grade. I want you to plan for something. Something big."

"Like a car?" asked Felipe.

"Or a trip?" asked Maria.

"Yes," said Ms. Sands. "Something that costs a lot. More than $500. That's the point. I will give you $500. You need to turn it into more. Don't just save it. Invest it."

"How?" asked Zach.

"Each of you will open an account at Sands Bank. You will decide where to put your money. You can go low risk …"

"What's that?" Zach asked.

"That's a savings account. Or a CD," said Ms. Sands. "Some bonds are low risk too. Or try high risk. Invest in mutual funds and stocks."

"When is it due?" asked Kate.

"At the end of the semester. We will make a chart. You will fill it out each week. It takes time to invest. To make money. So each week will count as a month."

Hands shot up. But Zoe wasn't listening. She was still daydreaming.

"Hold your questions," said Ms. Sands. "Go online. Do some research."

The class groaned.

"One more thing," said Ms. Sands. "How well you do counts toward your grade. Your grade can go up. It can go down. Just like the stock market! So be careful. Don't lose all your money."

"How will we know which stocks to choose?" asked Felipe.

"Take the time to learn," said Ms. Sands. "Some stocks will win. Some will lose. You must follow them. Every day. Just like it's real money. It's how you will learn."

After school, Zach and Zoe went home.
Zach was thinking about Ms. Sand's class.
"This econ project sucks," he said.

"Tell me about it," said Zoe. "I didn't get it!"

"Probably because you weren't listening,"
said Zach.

Zoe rolled her eyes. But she knew it was true.

Later, Zach talked to his best friend. Danny
was a year older.

"I had that class last year," said Danny.
"Your grade is riding on that project. So you
need a plan."

"Yeah," said Zach. "Where should I start?"

"That depends," said Danny. "Do you want to take a risk?"

"Heck, no, " said Zach. "I like sure things."

Danny laughed. "I know. Remember last year? We all went skydiving. You sat it out."

"The ground felt a lot safer," said Zach.

"Then go low risk. Start with a savings account. Check CD rates and terms," said Danny.

"That sounds good. Thanks, Danny. Talk to you later."

Zach hung up. He pulled up the Internet on his phone. He searched for CD rates. Zoe walked by. "Playing a new game?" she asked.

"I'm looking at bank rates," Zach said.

"Sounds like a total party," she said. "What the heck for?"

"For our econ assignment."

"My brother, the good student," Zoe laughed.

"You need to research too. The clock is ticking," said Zach.

"I'll just pick a stock I like."

"WHAT?!" yelled Zach.

Their parents heard Zach yell. "What's going on?" they asked.

"We have an econ project. The teacher is giving us fake money. We have to invest it. Zach doesn't like my idea," said Zoe.

"Because it's stupid!" said Zach.

"Zach!" said their dad.

"Sorry," said Zach. "But this is a big part of our grade."

"How do you start?" asked their mom.

"Choose our goal," said Zach. "What we're saving for. Something big."

"Okay," said their dad. "Zach, what do you want to buy?"

"A car," said Zach. "A used car. One with low miles."

"Zoe, what about you?" asked their mom.

"A trip. To the Amazon. Something wild. Somewhere I can bungee jump off a cliff."

"Why am I not surprised?" said Zach.

"I have an idea," said their dad. "There are games online. They teach you how to invest money."

"I like the sound of that," said Zoe.

"It couldn't hurt," said Zach.

A week went by. It was time to report in.

"Good morning," said Ms. Sands. "It's been one week. That means you have had your money for a month. Time to fill out the chart."

Zach came up. He wrote, "Opened savings account with $100."

Zoe came up. She had chosen a stock. She hadn't read much about it. But she liked the name. It sounded cool.

The students filled out the chart. "Now we will see if your money grows," said Ms. Sands.

Friday night Zach's phone rang.

"How's it going?" asked Danny.

"Good, dude. I'm still working on that econ thing," said Zach. "I've opened a savings account."

"Good start."

"I have to figure out what's next," said Zach.

"What about CDs?"

"I haven't put any money in one yet."

"The sooner the better. Longer term CDs pay more."

"You're right," said Zach. "I will sign up for a year."

"Okay," said Danny. "It's the weekend. Forget econ. Let's see who can get the best date."

Another week went by. Month two in project time. Zach's $100 savings made very little. He had put $200 in a CD. He chose a 12-month term. The money was earning more interest.

"Good job," said Ms. Sands. "You're spreading your money out. That is good. It's all slow growth. But it's steady."

Zoe checked her stock. It was up $20 a share. She smiled. "This isn't so hard," she said.

Two more weeks went by. It was dinnertime. Zach and Zoe sat down with their parents.

"How's the investing going?" asked their mom.

"I still have $200 to invest," said Zach.

"What about a bond?" asked their dad.

"Isn't that high risk?"

"It is an investment. But it's safer than stocks," said their dad.

"Bonds have terms. Like your CD," said their mom. "But they're longer. They earn more too."

"I'll check them out," said Zach.

"Zoe?" asked their dad. "How's your stock doing?"

"It's good," said Zoe. "It went up a couple of weeks ago."

"Did you check it this week?"

"Nah," said Zoe. "It's good."

Another week went by. "It's month five," said Ms. Sands. "Let's see how you are all doing. How much money have you made?"

Ms. Sands had computers in her classroom. The students checked the current interest rates. They checked mutual funds and stocks.

A cry came from the back of the room. "Oh no!"

"Zoe," said Ms. Sands. "Is everything okay?"

Zoe was upset. She had not been following her stock. She looked up from the computer. Ms. Sands went to her.

"My stock went down. I've lost half my money," she said.

Zoe was worried. Her grade would go down. She did not like losing. Especially to her brother.

"You put all your money in one stock," said Ms. Sands. "That was not a good idea. Why?"

"Because I could lose it all," said Zoe. "And it looks like I have. What should I do?"

"You might need to sell your stock."

"But I'll lose half my money," said Zoe.

"Yes, but you'll have half left. You can reinvest. Research it," said Ms. Sands.

That night, Zoe talked to her parents. "I blew it," she told them. "My stock crashed."

"Want to hear a story?" said her dad.

Zoe nodded.

"I was 23. I had just married your mom. We had a little money. I wanted more. A friend told me about a stock. I didn't look up its history. Your mom and I just bought some shares. It went up. We were excited. We stopped watching it."

"That was a mistake," said her mom. "It crashed. We lost it all."

"Stocks are high risk for a reason. You have to watch them," said her dad. "You have to be ready to sell."

"Stocks go up. They go down," said her mom. "They aren't like savings. They aren't like CDs."

"How can I fix this?" asked Zoe.

"Diversify," said her parents.

"What's that?" she asked.

"Spread your money out," said her mom. "Don't put it all in one place."

"Mutual funds," said her dad. "That's a good start."

"Many people put money in," said her mom. "Someone manages the fund. The money is used to buy stocks. It is used to buy bonds. Many types. Not all the same one."

"Oh," said Zoe. "So one could go up. Another might go down. But you won't lose all your money?"

"That's right," said her dad. "We will help you get started. Then you need to keep on top of it."

"Okay," said Zoe.

Three weeks later Zoe was the first up to the chart.

"How is your fund doing?" asked Ms. Sands.

"Great," said Zoe. "I have made back some of my money."

Zoe checked how Zach was doing. He was still making money. But it was only a little bit.

Weeks went by. It was almost the end of the semester. The projects were due.

Both twins had made money. Zach had made a little each week. Zoe had made back the money she lost. She had even started to make a bit more.

"I can't believe it," said Zach. "I could never have taken the risk you did. But it paid off. You figured it out."

"Thanks, Zach," said Zoe. "It was scary for a while. I get why you chose the safe way. And we both won. Our grades show that!"

Can making a plan to save lead to more money for you? Want to find out how to make a plan step-by-step and learn a little about low- and high-risk investment options?

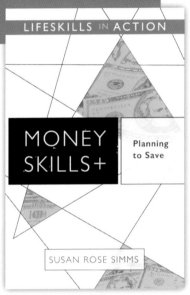

LIFESKILLS IN ACTION

MONEY SKILLS+

Planning to Save

SUSAN ROSE SIMMS

JUST *flip* THE BOOK!

LIFESKILLS IN ACTION
MONEY SKILLS

MONEY

Living on a Budget | Road Trip
Opening a Bank Account | The Guitar
Managing Credit | High Cost
Using Coupons | Get the Deal
Planning to Save | Something Big

LIVING

Smart Grocery Shopping | Shop Smart
Doing Household Chores | Keep It Clean
Finding a Place to Live | A Place of Our Own
Moving In | Pack Up
Cooking Your Own Meals | Dinner Is Served

JOB

Preparing a Résumé
Finding a Job
Job Interview Basics
How to Act Right on the Job
Employee Rights

SADDLEBACK
EDUCATIONAL PUBLISHING
www.sdlback.com

ISBN-13: 978-1-68021-013-2
ISBN-10: 1-68021-013-0
eBook: 978-1-63078-297-9

Printed in Malaysia

20 19 18 17 16   2 3 4 5 6

ACTION

MONEY SKILLS

Planning to Save

SUSAN ROSE SIMMS

Money.

You work hard to get it.

But it is easy to spend.

You eat out with friends.

Go to a movie. Buy a new shirt.

Before you know it, the money is gone.

What if you want something big?

A car. A trip. Money for college.

These cost a lot.

But you can get them.

You just have to **plan to save**.

How do you **save money**?

You set it aside. Don't spend it.

This seems easy. But it's not.

There is so much to buy.

Food. Clothes. School supplies.

And there are bills to pay.

Many people live paycheck to paycheck.

They earn money each month.

But they spend every penny.

Some even spend more than they make.

They want to save. But they don't.

Not saving can lead to big trouble.

Times can get tough.

People can lose their jobs.

Things can happen they don't expect.

A car accident. A hospital stay.

No savings means no money for times like these.

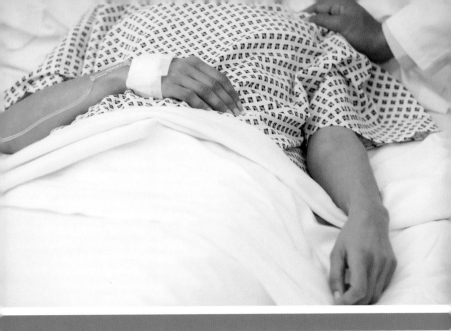

People go into **debt**. They owe others money.

They may lose things they have.

Their car. Even their home.

It is hard to get back on track.

That is why you must plan. Plan to save.

Anyone can save.

JUST FOLLOW THESE STEPS:

1. Set a goal.

2. Find money to save.

3. Treat savings like a bill.

First, **set a goal**.

What do you want to save for?

It could be a car. Or college.

Or a place of your own.

Write down how much you will need.

Set a date for reaching your goal.

It might be six months.

It might be a year.

It might be longer.

Now do the math.

How many months until you reach your goal?

Divide how much you need by the number of months.

This is what you must save each month.

Next, **find money to save**.

You know how much you need to save.

Subtract that number from what you make each month.

What is left?

There must be enough to pay your bills.

What if there is not?

You can still save.

But you will have to save less.

It will take longer to reach your goal.

What about things you want but don't need?

Game tickets. Eating out. Cable TV.

Cut back on these.

Then you can save more.

You will reach your goal faster.

Time for the last step.

Write down what you must save each month.

Treat savings like a **bill**.

Pay it each month.

You can get help with this.

Talk to your boss.

Part of your pay can go to savings.

Your bank can help too.

Money can go from checking to savings
each month.

You say how much.

You say which day.

The bank does the rest.

INVESTMENTS   BANK   MORTGAGES

You made a plan.

You are saving money.

But you can do more.

It is all about where you put your money.

There are many ways to save.

But there are **rules** for each one.

Find out which way is best for you.

You can go to a bank.

Or credit union.

Open a **savings account**.

This is a good way to start.

The money is out of your hands.

You are less likely to spend it.

You don't have to worry.

Your money is very safe.

The government protects it.

This is called **FDIC insured**.

Your bank may shut down.

But you will get your money.

Look for this when you open an account.

Ask about **interest rates** too.

Your money will earn more money.

It will not be much.

But you will get a little interest each month.

The higher the rate, the more money you earn.

Money in a savings account is safe.

It is also **liquid**.

This means you can take it out any time.

You will get a card.

You can use it to take money out.

Just go to an ATM machine.

Do you want to earn more money?

There are ways to do that.

But they are less liquid.

You can't take your money out for a while.

How long? It depends.

A CD is a **certificate of deposit**.

Most banks have CDs.

Your money is still safe. It is FDIC insured.

CDs have higher interest rates than savings accounts.

You earn more money.

But the money is not liquid.

You must have enough money to get a CD.

It might be $100. It might be more.

Ask your bank.

Choose the kind of CD you want.

It might be three months.

Or six months. Or a year.

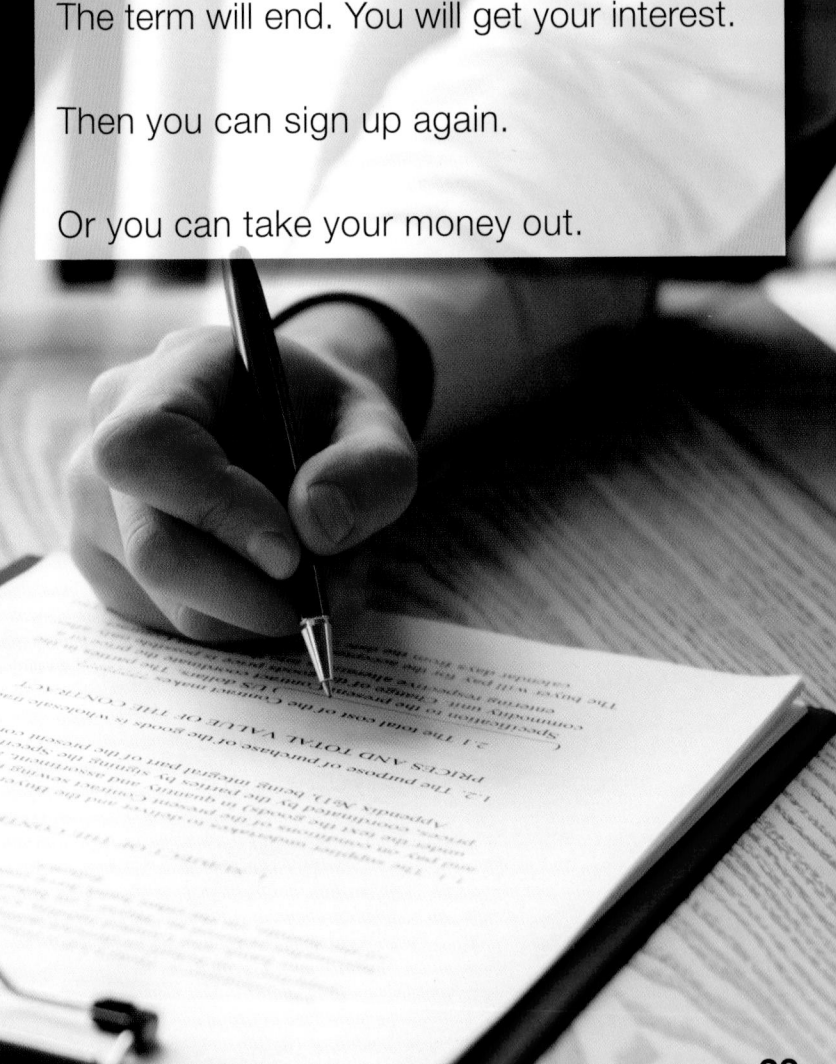

This is its **term**.

Your money stays in for that long.

The term will end. You will get your interest.

Then you can sign up again.

Or you can take your money out.

Can you wait five years to get your money?

Or even longer?

Then **invest**.

Use your money to make money.

Investing is about making money work for you.

You put your money in an account.

It stays there. You don't touch it.

It can be years.

But your money will grow over time.

There are safe ways to invest.

And there are risky ways.

Bonds are a safe way to invest.

Many are from the government.

Others are from companies.

Bonds are a way for them to borrow money.

You can buy bonds.

It is like lending money.

You are paid interest on that money.

Bonds have terms.

They work just like CDs.

The terms are longer.

The interest rates are higher.

Do you want to make even more money?

Are you willing to take a risk?

Then look into **stocks** and **mutual funds**.

Buying stock is like buying part of a company.

You can win big. But you can lose too.

It depends on how the company does.

You need to watch stocks.

Find out about companies.

Choose the ones you want to invest in.

Keeping up with stocks takes work.

You might want help.

Mutual funds give you that.

You put your money in. So do other people.

A person or company manages the fund.

The money is used to buy stocks and bonds.

You still need to look for good funds.

But you don't have to watch them as closely.

Saving money.

It takes work. It takes planning.

But it helps you reach your goals.

Your money can make more money.

And you have money when you really need it.

How much can you save?

Are you ready to invest?

Find out. Make a plan today.

JUST *Flip* THE BOOK!

Susan Rose Simms

Something
BIG

Which way of saving and investing is better? Zach and Zoe try to figure it out for their economics class in *Something Big*. Want to read on?